Chaotic Musings Vol 2
"Another round of applause"

Acknowledgement

We would like to acknowledge the true custodians of the land on which Radio Talk takes place, the Woiwurrung and Boonwurrung people of the Kulin Nation.

We acknowledge that treaties have never been signed and sovereignty was never ceded.
We cannot change the past so we must understand the negative impact that colonization has had upon the First Nations people.

It is important to understand and recognise that we at Vibe Union are lucky and privileged to put on an open mic every two weeks, where people are able to express themselves, tell their stories, when First Nations people in Australia have had their voices silenced and their stories untold throughout history, continuing to this present day.

As the MC of Radio Talk I would also like to acknowledge the Palawa people of Lutruwita since I was born and raised in Tasmania.

Illustrations by Pól the Painter

Preface

Hello everyone, Jason your poetic MC here, once again explaining what you are about to witness.

Chaotic Musings 2: The Musining (rejected title) is the much anticipated second installment of Vibe Union's poetry anthology series of poems from poets who have chosen to nestle themselves in the warm and unpredictable embrace that is Radio Talk poetry at Radio Bar.

As of writing, Vibe Union has now surpassed over three years of facilitating open mic poetry from countless individuals who have chosen to express themselves.
Under the supervision of the "Beefy Boys" those who come alone have been supported by Ry and myself who have kept the poetic party pumping perfectly, something we are proud of.

So sit back, have a cup of whatever liquid you desire, and enjoy this adventure of linguistic exploration.

Photos by Porsche Jansuwan
IG - @takenbyporsche

Contents

Acknowledgement		*ii*
Illustrations by Pól the Painter		*iii*
Preface		*iv*
Jason Voss (MC)	*RUOK?*	1
Izzy (Last Name Redacted)	*Silks*	7
K.S.K	*The Tapestry (1982)*	13
Vita Mia	*Vortex of Being*	17
Shyaire Ganglani	*Genocide is pretty simple.*	23
Mrsk	*Sonnet 1: Cronos*	31
Jemmi Ongom	*A Time to Be Alive*	33
Millaa Mercer	*The Sufi of Kolkata*	39
Gavi	*Matter & Mass*	47
KrakKen	*JUICE*	53
Xlvi Joon	*Imperfect*	55
Kairi Kerr	*Cowards & Cowboys*	59
Hayley	*Sewerslide*	63

Chris Jayawardena	*Forever Free*	73
Lane Milburn	*Hear a Change a Coming*	79
Farhana Muna	*Addict*	83
Amber Lette	*Lilac Trees...*	89
Yaru	*An Ode to Poop*	95
M.M. Salavatian	*Above The Barricade*	99
Girl with the Rose Tattoo	*Midnight*	103
Rhath	*Dogs at the Salt Flats*	105
Antonio Montaine	*Because we are lucky...*	109
Shua, the poet.	*Wanted*	113
Thank You		117

Jason Voss (MC)
IG - @user.name.unknown.jason

RUOK?

Jason Voss - RUOK?

RUOK?

Just Four letters right, that's easy

I mean I have at least 11 letters that I've been diagnosed with
Since Jesus decided to grant me the rhythm of the tism

How am I supposed to understand myself to answer those four stupid letters?

I sometimes don't understand soup

Like, is it a hot smoothie?
Then does that make a smoothie simply a cold fruit soup?
But you can get cold soup, gazpacho

So is a smoothie just a cold sweet soup or is a gazpacho a savoury smoothie?

Does putting vegetables in a smoothie make it a bastardised gazpacho or a hybrid sweet/savoury cold soup?

Jason Voss - RUOK?

Is tomato soup simply a warm fruit smoothie?

Also, if I put ice in my minestrone does that make it a chunky Italian smoothie or just cold soup?
An Italian bastardry of culinary criminality

What about a banana smoothie?
According to the internet and I quote:

'Bananas are both a fruit and not a fruit'
'It's actually an herb distantly related to ginger'

A more important question lingers here:
Why the fuck do I care so much?

Why does the idea of soup permeate the entirety of what sits inside my skull?

RUOK???

No

Jason Voss - RUOK?

How am I supposed to be ok when soup makes me angry and confused?

There are 5 letters in 'Segue'

Are we to merely sit and wait for this one approved day a year with fingers crossed, on tenterhooks, with bated breath and filled with anticipation for someone, for anyone, to say those four sweet sweet juicy letters in which we can finally feel comfortable about being honest with what is truly happening inside our minds

Jargonistically oversharing in a blaze of horrific and glorified vulnerability, rising from the ashes like a weird screeching neurospicy phoenix with profound awkwardness

Jason Voss - RUOK?

Is 364 days of relentlessly thinking about soup and the ideology surrounding the entirety of the culinary discipline all A-Okay if we can rely on a cup of tea and a doughnut at work to show that:
'We like to give the impression we care about those with mental health issues but refuse to alter any aspect of how we conduct ourselves professionally to facilitate change, shut up, have another doughnut and most importantly, get back to work'

Is the second Thursday in September the mental health Christmas?

Do I mark it on my sexy firefighter calendar that a depressed and anxious Santa will awkwardly not drink any milk nor taste a cookie in the fear of feeling bad for taking someone else's food from their own house?

Jason Voss - RUOK?

Overthinking about whether or not he should have consumed at least something because he doesn't want the effort to go unappreciated, leaving a magic note behind in hopes to smooth things over and quell the existential dread he now finds himself in

A note that simply reads:

RUOK?

No

And now I want soup

Izzy (Last Name Redacted)

IG - @littleizzyruth

Silks

Izzy (Last Name Redacted) - Silks

Pink are the shoes
I had no money and
no business
in buying.
White are the pills I take
so that I can pretend
I am trying.
Translucent are the tears
that cascade
when I am crying.
Red is the flash of blood
when I have
a lust for dying.

Purple is my hair
that I colour to feel alive.
Orange is my car
I no longer care to drive.
Sallow olive, my skin
that I cover in ink.
Clear is the drink
for when I no longer
wish to think.

Izzy (Last Name Redacted) - Silks

Rosy are the cheeks and
brunette are my brows.
My bank card flashes grey
for when my pension allows.

Envy-coloured green,
my favourite hue.
Scarlett-coloured letters,
the bills overdue.
Blue is how I feel
almost all of the time.
Yellow is the bile,
dry-retching,
heave, chyme.

Sable is the fawn.
My predisposed phase.
A tangerine dawn
From atop the mountains,
pretty blaze.

Izzy (Last Name Redacted) - Silks

And black are the nights
that really never end.
Lime in my soda.
Gold hardware.
Silver sealed letters
that I don't send.

Brown is the desk
upon which I don't write,
about bone coloured bones.
Out of mind,
out of sight.
Cerulean-tinged skies
where in my sleep
I take flight.
Laced with sapphire veins,
that run course
through my might.

Izzy (Last Name Redacted) - Silks

And I,
and I.
I once did fight.
Adorned with bruises
coloured umber.
Loud
were the drips of ruby,
the times I was torn
asunder.

But I await the rebirth -
Peach ass, apricot lips.
Deliverance from the womb.
Cardinal rips and
straight to
liqueur amber sips.

Izzy (Last Name Redacted) - Silks

And to live is lavender,
in a field of my family.
With orchids of crimson.
The shade my smile should be.
A salmon grimace and
chestnut eyes.
Charcoal thoughts and
champagne lies.
A vermilion stained death,
but at the very least, I tried.
Flax or fuchsia,
lilac or saffron,
please,
wrap me in silk on the day I die.

K.S.K
Kerstin Singh-Kurz

K.S.K, also known as Kerstin Singh-Kurz, was a mixed-media visual artist born in Australia to German immigrants in the 1960's. Throughout her life she balanced her creative pursuits with working for various media and editing companies. Following the birth of her only child in the 1990's, Kerstin largely withdrew from her artistic endeavors, keeping most of her works private. Facing multiple health challenges, she continued to grapple with the torment of living a life as a creative. Kerstin passed away in 2016, leaving behind a legacy of art and creativity. Eight years after her death, it was revealed that she was also a talented writer and poet, with her works slated for posthumous publication. Her artistic legacy lives on through her child, Izzy (Last Name Redacted).

The Tapestry (1982)

She sews stitches of splendour
handcrafting her figure
into the art's centre
among seasons of embroidered men
in pastel shades
of herringbone and satin
working in the memories
that meant the past to her

She spends her youth weaving into hours
creating her very life in this art
and finally, completing the craft
with a border of her favourite flowers

The tapestry complete in marvel
hangs gracefully in her air
she is now ready to taste the world
which lay forbidden out there

She passes her days on the outside
as she passes through her lovers
she makes no time for tears of pity
she knows no fear for the height of the city
and she faces the illusions
as harmful intrusions
she insists she has a mission to fulfill
her tapestry, her tale
created in skill

K.S.K - The Tapestry (1982)

For after each season she breathes
each man she destructively leaves
she returns to the tapestry
still proudly hung
unpicking each stitch
which made up a man
carefully one by one

The seasons did go as quick as the sorrows
and she raises the tapestry
which held the threads of tomorrows
high into the sunlight gazing to her figure
remaining alone in the art's centre
in shades of lavender her favourite colour
all the seasons unpicked
even the lavender has frayed
and she knows it is time
to end the game she has played
she folds the tapestry
to be admired again never
locking it away
in a carved box
forever

Vita Mia
IG - @wordhungerblog

Vortex of Being

Vita Mia - Vortex of Being

Hindsight

Into state of mind

Rewind

To reshape the past

Viewed thrvough mirror rather than glass,

To reflect.

I normally deflect

The in-depth questions

But persistence

And conversations

Build resilience.

I insist

On my part in the matter.

The glass of illusion shatters

And fragmented is the future

A kaleidoscope of vision

The light scattered

Into dark corners.

Illuminated decisions

Driven only by our existence

And what is to come of it.

Vita Mia - Vortex of Being

Blinded by the truth

But wrapped in its warmth,

The heat envelops

The shadows of our being

And black reflects all colour.

To fall into the void

Is to paint the soul

And where colours bleed and boundaries blur

Passion resides.

To touch the flames is to breathe,

To succumb to its fire

Is to live.

Shyaire Ganglani

IG - @shyreesays

Genocide is pretty simple.

Shyaire Ganglani - Genocide is pretty simple.

Say it one more time,

It's complicated,

How are we meant to know,

Who are we to pick a side?

It's all just so complicated

Algebra is complicated

Avril Lavigne is complicated

Middle-aged mortgage people

Who whinge about the economy

Are complicated

The way my father was good to us

But bad for the people he ruined

Is complicated.

Shyaire Ganglani - Genocide is pretty simple.

A 75-year genocide is a lot of things,

Infuriating

Terrifying

Heartbreaking

Blood-curdling

Nightmare inducing

And some how so predictable

History does not just repeat itself

People with too much power write it

Read that again

History does not just repeat itself

People

with

too

much

power

rewrite it

Shyaire Ganglani - Genocide is pretty simple.

Don't let them fuel a fire they started

With another matchstick

Say it. Go on. One more time.

Televise your cowardice

Toe another precipice

The world is watching while you say

It's controversial

Controversial is a cop-out

Controversial is whitewashing

Rainbow painting black facing

Moral debasing nonsense

Controversial is men who get away with

Fraud, shaming, assault, rape and literal murder

Only to be temporarily out of order

Like a vending machine that's out of water

Till they're restocked,

Shyaire Ganglani - Genocide is pretty simple.

After a public apology tour,

Controversial is her

Controversial is me too

It's a hashtag with an expiry date

It's a pay gap so wide

We're all falling for it

Controversial is coloniser math

It's calling it an eye for an eye

Then taking the whole corpse

Controversial is not children

Discovering Babas mangled bodies

Under cement homes

THAT is not controversial

Say it one more time

It's touchy

Touchy is a subject

Shyaire Ganglani - Genocide is pretty simple.

Not what matters

It's your creepy uncle

Your problematic boss

The pope with too much power

And not enough accountability

Touchy is asking a mature lady her age

It's your mate's questionable jokes at the pub

Touchy is stepping on cultural toes

And asking "does that hurt?"

Touchy is not children's drawings on missiles

Shot into the sky

Like a fridge magnet letter of destruction

It is not touchy.

Shyaire Ganglani - Genocide is pretty simple.

When empathy is a metaphor

And promises are empty and

Promise lands with olive trees

Are as it stands

Hollow of hope.

Take your moral compasses

And hold it to the heavens,

And beg for re-calibration,

Behind the shadows where your excuses hide

Just stop.

Stop with your selective politeness

Stop with your euphemisms

Stop with your who and how and whataboutism

Shyaire Ganglani - Genocide is pretty simple.

Call this what it is

call this what it is

Call this what it is

Murder. Genocide. Holocaust. Apartheid.

Do not turn the page,

Do not change the channel,

Turn your blind eyes into a crystal ball,

And vow out loud.

Never. Again.

Mrsk

Sonnet 1: Cronos

Mrsk - Sonnet 1: Cronos

She reels the seconds in upon her line,
Green amaranth entwining her grey head;
Her wrinkled brow and crows' feet wink and shine,
And sky-blue eyes infinity portend.
Her fine long fingers turn and spin the dials,
She patiently as any titan sets
The watch to run; once more the sun to climb,
And all God's earth to turn she kindly lets.
Into this palace, children come and go,
Sit on her lap, enchanted, minutes play;
There hail and thunder, here a sparkling throne
(A rust-red stool), the oil lamp's flick'ring glow.
Oh Watchmaker, one day you too shall lie
Forever silent, then all time shall die.

Jemmi Ongom

IG - @jemmigawjus

A Time to Be Alive

My creators

What a time to be alive!
Feel this shift   in your life
Let it   light up   your spirit
Hold this solar heat,
Shadow box at your own pace,
Move, dance, spin

to your own beat!
Breathe in
Taking in all the blue sky serenity,
Feels so heavenly
Body aware sensually

heaviness and its tangled knotty bits,
Sweating out the losses
With each drip
   Drip
   Drip
   Drip
Out of the tap
I let go
Any reactions to
     The mind's disrespect

This is my truth
real and authentic
Caramel brown love is poppin
Mocha soul glow is rockin
Giving big hugs to
 my lonely thoughts
The happiness....
I believed... I didn't deserve...
Feeling and rubbing
all my bouncing curls
Skippin and laughin

by the soft wind
I watch

 young black boys

and

 young black girls
     Sangin out loud:
    We are the world!

And make no mistake

we ain't gonna

shrink, shake or break
        not even some crude dude

in a rude mood

    Miss me!
with that attitude!
We raising these
    bodies of healing vibrations
  Spreading   ripples   across
    collective   elevations

    Inviting this here
My   inner   matter   I   exude
i feel you

I Feel YOU

I   FEEL   YOU

I see you

I See YOU

I   SEE   YOU

I   ACCEPT   YOU

Jemmi Ongom - A Time to Be Alive

One   day
At a time
Counting   your peace
Cos today   feels   closer
The freedom
          Of   being   Alive

    This   BE
My   daily   gratitude.

Millaa Mercer

YT - @thekajalflaneur

The Sufi of Kolkata

Millaa Mercer - The Sufi of Kolkata

A tale of love and limerence, simple poems of bitter surrender

Dohe

Our, love is a bed of blackened roses in spring breeze, which turn out to be green carnations in a winter storm.

We, ghosts of the future, you sunburnt, I moonlit.
Fornicating against some dark void, our entwining the definition of extinction.

Yet, what connects us is a bridge of sighs - yours of breathless moans, mine of depthless cries.

If only you could see me as something other than: white, noble, fragile. We could bask in the starlight of endless affection.

Instead, I'll write these paltry ghazals in water...

Millaa Mercer - The Sufi of Kolkata

Ghazal no. 1

I hear the autumn rain fall, like leaves crushed underfoot.
The cyber city sparkles from your foggy window.
Your eyes in the dark are diamonds in the soot night sky.

You lay, a tired Prince resting, upon a bed like a marble grave
Sheets of cotton and silk, a plastic sea beneath your ceiling sky
A mirage of time in front of me,
Sweet mono-brow, caramel skin delight
Rich migrant lover, the black rose of my night
Slowly falling affection, a pebble slipping off a cliff into the dark ravine below.
The sound of whirling dervishes and jazz fill the air tonight.

He, from gold and marble palaces in old Kolkata, me, from an open sewer by the seaside.
All I see is a glass ceiling, what he calls a concrete floor, it's my sky shimmering.

Millaa Mercer - The Sufi of Kolkata

Ghazal no. 2

Kind One, it's your name on my tongue, it's sweetness burns like liquid agony.
Hollowing out an ache in my bones, only emptiness courses through these airy veins to nourish the baseless vault of my heart.
Kind One, let me dream of sweet content or die, and so forget what love ever meant,
Roses growing in the snow of my disappointment and discontent. Is my love bitter honey or poison milk?
This twilight of false idols and stolen moments fade gently.

I pray five times a day for you, to look at me, the same way you glimpse the moon behind the sun.
I freeze yet burn since from myself to you I turn.

Now, I surrender to your multiplicity under the mirrors of the Mughals.
At once under your spell, and aware of it also.
My love is a dreamscape of misplaced desire in pure cinema.

Millaa Mercer - The Sufi of Kolkata

My loneliness turned to vinegar at the electric
eyes of your rejection, unfeeling ignorance, the
face which turns to a golden mask of
cosmopolitan indifference.

Your coldness so tender to my soul,
Pulsating like a snakes heart on the table,
Sold for a click, a like, some fleeting gesture of
anonymous sycophancy.

I surrender to all of this, no longer fight it.

Like Shiva dancing in the viridian flames,
Kind One!
You are my Sufi of Kolkata,
forevermore.

Gavriel Dorota ach'é'é Yonathan dóó Helena Bashishchiin Hashk'ąą hadzohi

IG - @triple.cat.art

Matter & Mass

Gavriel Dorota - Matter & Mass

I always wanted to redefine gravity
the sense of this non-entity, the being
binding all of us together
not quite conveyed
miscommunication of severity
causes us to drift away

molecular bonds to break
family ties to fray, sever
moons flung & tides settle.

I've been told Jupiter
is Earth's big brother
taking meteoric hits & swinging
the rest back to obscurity,
from cold scrutiny they came.

I think this is another case study
in ageism & scientific misogyny.
Two incorrect assumptions:
gender;
birth order.
I think Jupiter is me.

Gavriel Dorota - Matter & Mass

Bloated gas giant, particles held under duress
that would crush any would be astronaut.
Others ponder—in earshot—about how
I must be ready to burst, to blow under pressure.
I'm told I all storm, no quiet
but I'm quite certain the red
effectively sequestered to ire of an eye
in which my mortal form
which fit trillions of times over.
Still, I dip pen into those mists,
dance with trials of tragedy,
the after effects, lingering wisps on each step.

Some days I apologise about the volume of my
Ex meaning:
- the space consumed,
- & loudness in my head.

You say I don't have to
    —I do
for all the rocky landings
your rovers received.

Gavriel Dorota - Matter & Mass

I had cast his lot into the Styx.
I'd hoped he'd drown,
made his ghost impervious, everlasting,
but I know how to bring Achilles to heel.
Snap the baton of the maestro:
orchestra stops;
the trauma of the waltz halted.

I want you to understand the gravity of this
'sorry'.
No more low-pressure fronts rolling in
nor subsequent leaden rain.
Please, take shelter beneath my clouds
as protection from cosmic rays.

I sold my weddings rings
at a run-down pawn shop;
used the funds for a telescope
that might peer beyond all the past.

Gavriel Dorota - Matter & Mass

I gifted my wigs
to a trans clothing swap;
where one wore a Commandment,
another found liberation.

I tore strips from scarves
to amend the burns
from plasma streaking sky
& evoking tears down cheeks.

I always wanted to redefine gravity;
I couldn't yet, because I didn't know
how much you'd mean.

KrakKen

IG - @krakk3n8

JUICE

KrakKen - JUICE

JUICE
Don't test me, I can't be held Liable
Their style's lukewarm oppressed Minimal
I have a request at least
try serve it raw to these Individuals
but their self control's Intolerable
Who's the best, that's Debatable
I'm just here to make it Relatable
All them jerks are the Bait-Ables
With nothing new but Recyclables
Go recite something Reliable
They're fronting just to excite the New
Some of them sometimes are alright
but need to be more Knowledgeable
Burnt out nothing much except a Few
Watered down subjects without the Juice*
Their whole style's suspect and Overdue
It's old now un-fresh topic of News!
When I drop it I Expect nothing less
Totally I rock it I rep it
and wear it out like my Tattoos..

Xlvi Joon

Imperfect

Xlvi Joon - Imperfect

I'm not afraid of imperfections. I see them and I love them still.

I am afraid for you to see them, knowing that in time you will.

So I sense a time together to hide prior to pumpkin hour,

to avoid that brutal moment where admiration begs to sour.

This makes me stop myself each time from vulnerable straight display,

fearful that my genuine self will cause in you hurtful dismay.

By keeping myself from receiving the acceptance of my flaws,

I grow and nurture this fear further, turn the effect into its cause.

I desperately want to break this cycle stuck on full repeat,

but the pain keeping me stuck wants to be the pain I breed.

Xlvi Joon - Imperfect

I want to hate myself right for it, disgust myself in growing shame,

repel myself and those that love me, pointing, appointing to them blame.

I have to make the sound decision to love myself no matter what

in order to attract acceptance and the love I never got.

Kairi Kerr

IG - @mirrors_on_mirrors

Cowards & Cowboys

Kairi Kerr - Cowards & Cowboys

Good person, identity ungraspable
A quicksand, running though clasped capital
The more attached   the further passed
Pull turned push,   a magnetic reversal,
poetically tired to one, ironically self prophetic

Any mistake leaving one heaving to
hold to, sand grains in plywood cracks that cry, "good",
                                                                       "great
If missteps inescapable, we've left to pay double
Shedding cost to victim, would you kill for a clean slate

Attaching to good, bad, so easy, so reductive
Knowing each held both the harmed and harmer
Knowing each keep both the harmed and harmer
Splitting to good, bad, too easy, too redundant

The very first analysis, slices whole to two
Ivory and ebony de-merge, cut with knife forged not void
of bias, as no straight lines can be drawn
                                      with such human of hands

Lines made via hot blade, scaffold and braid,
the sum and its parts

Kairi Kerr - Cowards & Cowboys

If not good, not bad. If behaviour doesn't justify how we identify,
God, why
                are you such. a fucking. asshole.

I think
    maybe
        the good people, aren't good
I think
    maybe
        they're the brave ones
I think we mean,
        the brave ones

Because it's easy, isn't it. To recoil from first blood shed,
Shout "bleeding heart" at anyone left on the field while fled
Retreat, run 'n build, build and repress
call a dark room and pale, unscarred skin - success

Now when he screams,
    he looks like the small dogs i pity
Furious from forced shedding
    of their wolven beginning

Kairi Kerr - Cowards & Cowboys

And scared. So scared, by a world so scalably larger, so grim
A world that twisted its tail, made it hard to inhale, all for an aesthetic downscale
A world so bluntly uncontrollable, moved at leash, at whim

I see fear behind all your lashing bites
I wish you asked us
I wish you knew,
              how scared we were too

Hayley

IG - @whatrickowrote

Sewerslide

Hayley - Sewerslide

He awakens
It's a sluggish start
Most days a struggle
To peel himself from a sleepless night
The sun a distant reminder of where
Night stops
And nothing else.

                                        He gathers
                                          He hunts
                                    For belongings
                          Crowds them into a backpack

                        Leaves

And he
Moves swiftly now
The bus waits for no one
And he picks up pace
An energy he never expects
And just in time
He sees the 158 approach.

                    Stuck between passengers who are
                      Stuck between other passengers
                          He keeps earphones in
                            To feel himself carried

                          Away

Hayley - Sewerslide

But here
In this space
When he doesn't expect it
Doesn't want it
The music stops
          The beat
                    Stops.

A thought catches

          In his throat

A blackness shuts him inside

               His own

                   Mind.

                      The bus feels like a

                          Prison

           Or maybe
           On the

        Way

Hayley - Sewerslide

To a prison, he can't –

Understand.

        Why he's here.

And the bus dings as it lands him
At chosen destination
And he feels his feet pick himself up out of the –

                And he walks off the bus
                He breathes the air
                And keeps moving.

*

She wakes restlessly
Not sure if she wants to rise or fall back to sleep
Neither seem preferable
Why can nowhere feel comfortable?

                But sigh and shrug
                It's not so bad
        She drags a sleepless body from the sheets
                Thinking here I am
                It's alright, I found me

Taking comfort in the ritual of toast and juice
And she moves and –

        As she walks

Hayley - Sewerslide

As she moves through the new day
Her thoughts

Entangle

Freeze.

And the momentum

Dies.

Water is clogged

In

Her

Brain, and she –

Feels it

Run

Forcefully

To her

Eyes.

Hayley - Sewerslide

How can a –

An undefined –

Thought, be

So

Destructive.

How can

Nothing

Make you want to –

Cry?

Hayley - Sewerslide

Snap
Out of it
Here we are now
Like a mouse in a wheel, she's
Found her footing
And she avoids the thoughts
All of them
Because what do they do anyway?
What do they really do?

*

Neither he nor she really clutch at a diagnosis
Because what can that say

       A label covers the box but doesn't make you
                              want to look inside

Feelings don't really listen to labels in any case
They move and prod of their own volition

                    But life is a gift –
                    Right?

Sometimes she thinks it's a gift she didn't ask for
And doesn't deserve

       Sometimes he thinks it's a gift that doesn't fit
                         And he should return

And maybe he isn't he

                                  And she isn't she

                Maybe they are both me

Hayley - Sewerslide

Or you
    But really

        Maybe

They are just them
Which is just us
The voices that will catch in your throat
As you resist the urge to cry out

Forever terrified of not hearing the echo
Whisper back in the dark -

You are not alone.

Chris Jayawardena

IG - @harrington_35

Forever Free

Chris Jayawardena - Forever Free

Free,
What is free ?

Someone please teach me,
What in this world is truly free ?

If you aren't paying for it, doesn't that make you the product ?

You see,
We live in a world where silicon valley reigns supreme over people's minds.

Making billions by altering your brain chemistry,

Tell me,
Do you like being reduced to a number on a data registry ?

Rehabs for addiction & here we are, walking around with potent drugs held tight against our skin.

With notification sounds that play in your head, like hammer pounding on tin.

Oh look, its dopamine on demand. !!

Chris Jayawardena - Forever Free

What is forever,
Is it just another word for infinity ?

Math makes it easy,
Divide anything by zero and you will find it.

So if there's nothing truly free
&
If nothing lasts forever.

What do I mean, when I say,
I want to live forever free.

It is to live each day without feeling the weight of the world on my chest.

It is being content with knowing I gave all I did my best.

It is the ability to have a conversation with another, without it feeling like a test.

It is the wisdom to know when my body and mind needs to rest.

It is the blowing of the wind as I sway to the rhythm of the music.

Chris Jayawardena - Forever Free

It is laughing with my mates till the sides of my belly hurt.

It is being able to laugh at my lowest, rolling around in the dirt.

It is finding joy, even in what I consider to be work.

It is being kind to one another, never a jerk.

It is walking tall, even if around the corner demons & monsters may lurk.

It is a freeing from past trauma

It is the grin on your face, eating a post party 2am chicken shawarma.

It is being content, knowing that justice will be delivered by Karma.

To be forever free,
Is what I wish to be.

From the mountains, down to the sand by the sea.

I will fall on my knees & yell out.

That I will find peace and balance each day,
No matter whether the skies are blue or
they may be gray.

...
......
....

Lane Milburn

IG - @lunarlane

Hear a Change a Coming

Lane Milburn - Hear a Change a Coming

I hear there's a change coming.
I hear that there's a future coming,
against all odds.
I hear there's a train going to a setting
where there's a story starting and I'm betting
that there's gonna be a change coming
with a strange main plot.

I hear there's a conversation happening.
That there are people whispering behind street
corners who are trying to keep their voices
down,
that there are dreamers who are imagining
a transformation of second chances
in the glistening decisions and choices that I
hear are coming round.

I hear that they're selling Keep Cups for coffee
in cafes in Fitzroy.
That customers are speaking up when they
order lattes
and swapping their milk out for conscientious
caffeine with soy.
I hear that recycling is all the rage now.
That the resources are running low
and that the dollars don't count,
that the next chapter in our history
has to factor in the mystery
of no trees for paper to write on when the
pages start running out.

Lane Milburn - Hear a Change a Coming

I hear the bars are putting Molotovs on the
cocktail menus,
and that the people are shouting rounds
of a new flavour of shots.
That they're looking for a venue to start
housing the creators in
who make music in the sounds of an artist
army lead response.

I hear that there's a room full of people who
want to listen.
That there's a stage and a microphone and a
space where we can talk,
about a change they hear a coming
and the transition they envision,
and where it goes when they're caught
between a hard place and an even harder rock.

I hear that they're afflicted with existence,
they're sending letters and signing petitions,
that there's a room full of writers who have
stories they haven't written.
And I hear that the people have put their ears
to the ground,
because they hear that change is coming
but they're worried that they're the only ones
who can hear the sound.

Farhana Muna

Addict

Farhana Muna - Addict

Used you like a drug
Called it my fairy-tale love
Put you in a needle
Then shot you up my skin
Let the nervous system disruption begin

Your teeth claw at my veins
I bruise and bleed
recreate that childhood pain
Which makes me like you when you treat me like shit
And make you love me, because I put up with it

You show up at my door again
fire off whispers loaded with my name
I pour you gin mixed with apple juice
You'll lie to me to the whole night and then blame it on the liquor
Hate fucking is my preferred gold sticker
for being the perfect addict
For letting you prick holes
all over my body
Until I'm sinking like the titanic

Farhana Muna - Addict

You leave, it's been 4 hours since your last call
Panic rising, anxious in my attachment
My love isn't ruled by Venus, but by the fear of abandonment
I can't breathe - fuck what did I do now?
Have you been in a car accident or is this another punishment?
Then I remember
You're on a date with another woman
Handing out your "love" like it's a Christmas giveaway

Call you a dozen times, begging you to pick up
my critical thinking has left the chat
With trembling fingers
I send you text after text
Fighting, fleeing, freezing simultaneously - amygdala hijack
Oh god, has he left me again?

Farhana Muna - Addict

I'm no longer a grown woman who can think straight
Back to being a 10 year old
Watching dad fight with mama while he packs his bags
I plan to throw myself at his feet,
cling on to his legs, block the doorway
beg and plead
convince him, "Please. Please don't leave."

Because people who love you, stay.
You finally reply, "call you in 10"
I exhale
It's been 40 minutes
The fear of abandonment,
Bubbling up my throat as vomit

Are they kissing, touching and already naked in bed?
Someone yank this film reel playing in my head.

Farhana Muna - Addict

I want to call my best friend.
But I am ashamed.
I told her I was over him.
Serves me right to feel alone in this.
I deserve every bit of the suffering
Because I chose 'other' over being wise

I curl up in foetal position
Dear god, "Save. Me."
And I'm not even religious
It must've worked, angels with a pulse showed up
Checked me into emotional rehab
Held me through every withdrawal
Healed me with their kindness, grace and kicked my ass
Poured Dettol on my cuts and bubble wrapped my falls

Farhana Muna - Addict

There's still steps left in the recovery program
Pacing the precipice of relapse,
cravings haven't gone away
I try to recreate your embrace
around the contours of my rib cage
Stare at my phone,
Tempted to return your 6th missed call from
Monday
and say, "Okay, fine. I'm ready to be friends again."

But that's not gonna happen,
I'm in detox
Donald trump, leopard's spots
and your broken character - some things never change

So I'll pass on the syringe,

decline your offerings of love

This is no fairy tale,

we're just addicts, using the same drug

Amber Lette

Lilac Trees and Crimson Dusk to my Love

Amber Lette - Lilac Trees and Crimson Dusk

Lilac trees and crimson dusk
Cherry blossoms and satin silk vision that
leaves one feeling mesmerized.
The road to enchantment and mystical vision.
Purple euphoria and the sphere of magenta.
The bold flames of carmine red implode into
the wild depths of ruby.
In the rust of the flashing glowing lights of
floating sapphires.
The visionary of imperfections floating and
swimming among the stars.
The crimson dusk's equivalence amounts to
absolutely nothing.
To love to lust to desire.
The hurricane ruby downfall.
Lilac ribbons and orange dust fall from the moon.
The autumn leaves and the tapestry of autumn
rain, and the cherry blossoms are brought
back to life through the magenta haze and
reflections.

Amber Lette - Lilac Trees and Crimson Dusk

Of the crystal blue flowing ocean at dawn.
Sunset at midnight.
Twilight floats leisurely through the trees.
Let there be no despair.
Luscious deep shades of magenta everywhere.
Carmine red lives on as my fragmented heart bleeds for crimson and lilac melt as a deep breeze sets in
It's fall once again. It's fall once again.
The crimson perspective of the gold leaves in the Devine office.
Opium and ecstasy in the carnal breeze
My love letters go unsent.
Love is gold
My heart bleeds turquoise as I drown in an ecliptic vision

Yaru

IG - @yaru_himself

An Ode to Poop

Yaru - An Ode to Poop

Take a dump my friend,
Just do it, mate!
It's the best thing you can do,
right in this moment,
Trust me.

It can get hard, real fast.
Some sort of Shite-land cement,
Hydro-turd if you ask me.
Give it a night and then the next day,
Comes the sun and its all yellow
No brown,
Until it's all black again.

A mere few repetitions of this somewhat mundane pallete and then,
I shall guarantee thee my fair friend,
Thou shall be amazed at the extent of sacrifices willfully made to the ceramic altar,
Just to bury the demons under.
And watch as he, the almighty God of constipation (poop be upon him),
gracefully and miraculously,
Resets your priorities,
Quicker than any enlightened Shaman,
Guru or Therapist,
could ever imagine.

Yaru - An Ode to Poop

Have some prunes and
Take a mighty dump champ,
right now,
It's the best thing you can do.
Trust me.

M.M. Salavatian
Above The Barricade

Foreword by Yaru

"While writing my poem for the first Poets for Palestine fundraiser, I remembered fractions from one of the many wartime stories my father had told us as kids, from his time at the battlefront of the Iran-Iraq war during the 1980s. A story of a bird flying over the war zone.

After the first PFP event, I asked him to refresh my memory about that story and it turns out that he actually wrote it as a short poem during his time of service! The poem, for me at least, resembles a first-hand record of the absurdity of war through the lens of those who despite having to be at the forefront of it, want nothing from it, but for it to end.

This is a poem about a bird that my father, who was then a wartime private, had noticed flying over their heads while he and the rest of his Iranian comrades were holding a barricade against Iraqi forces during a hot summer day somewhere in Southern Iran.

Originally written in Farsi, I asked whether I could translate it, and was then able to perform it at the second Poets for Palestine fundraiser."

- Yaru, Arash Salavatian

M.M. Salavatian - Above the Barricade

The bird,
Calm, beautiful and enchanting,
Spread its wings.
Underneath the scorching cool blue sky
As if it was swimming in a golden sea of rays,
Over our heads.

The spectators,
A swaying bush dancing to the soothing
rhythm of waves,
A skylark leading a choreography of
riverbanks,
A colourful butterfly
Circling the velvety shrine of red poppies
As the purest of dews
Stitches the flower and the morning breeze
together in unison.

You and me, however,
Desperately tired, sit on the opposite sides of
this barricade we've made.
With our snow-white hearts and blood red
hands,
Eyes glimmering with hope,
While staring at a grey ocean of despair.
A gunmetal sorceress with a necklace made of
lead,
scorned eyes lined with soot,
That are locked on our destiny.

M.M. Salavatian - Above the Barricade

Oh,
You wretched summoners of war!
I saw it, with my own eyes,
All that his eyes could see.
We watched it together with love,
How a bird could fly,
This iconic act of liberation,
Moved us both, equally,
And I'm sure I saw love in the eyes of the bird
And I'm sure it saw it in ours too,
Equally.

But are you patient enough to observe,
how equal is the joy of gazing at liberation
being shared?

While you, anxious sea-folk,
On-board of a split Titanic,
Forever restrained vampires of doom,
Await your forever forbidden grace.

Bare the unbearable weight of eternal shame!
For the harder you try
To conquer beauty,
The uglier you become.

Mir Mohammad Salavatian
Jan 1983

Girl with the Rose Tattoo

Midnight

Girl with the Rose Tattoo - Midnight

You are a sunrise
While I'm a sunset
You feel like dew on a fresh morning
And I am the change in the air as the sun
goes down
Together we were midnight
The in between
But Just like midnight
We were never meant to last
Just howl at the moon till it set into the morning
filling the world with dew once more

Rhath

IG - @rhath_music

Dogs at the Salt Flats

Rhath - Dogs at the Salt Flats

Rabid dogs stand at the edge of salt flats
Lapping for water in what blood they can find
Blood that speckles red on the crystals
And stains **black** on the dirt

The hounds hold their heads low to the oppresive cloud cover
A ceiling on all tomorrows

The salt has cured our flesh; it will keep

Dogs feed 'til sundown
Then they will hunt one another

….

**[Reports show a clear cause of the salination
Redacted, then released. No matter]**

```
Psychological factors in target selection
```
To put the fear of our god in 'em
Or make them believe we're him

At very least, capture images to show back home.
Scattered limbs and lines erased from history.

Rhath - Dogs at the Salt Flats

[Reports show a clear cause of the salination]

The peninsula still smoulders
All but forgotten
Sticky fire. Hells inferno as a wash across a landscape and their skin.

[Reports show a clear cause of the salination]

`"We are fighting against human animals,"`
came an echo upon stained marble.
Repeated again and again on a western gale wind.
White phosphorous and rubble, like before and again, salt the earth.

...

Rabid dogs stand at the edge of salt flats
At the edge of no tomorrows
Dining on cured meat until sundown

Antonio Montaine

IG - @antoniomontaine

Because we are lucky enough to have sisters

Antonio Montaine - Because we are lucky enough to have sisters

We named our wooden horses Castor and Pollux

Held hands in bed ushering in manufactured freedom

Our fingers interlocked strong chain link DNA

Holding back the monsters in the next room

Words the keys to the locks that kept us safe

I sat next to you as we rode dirty sheets across impossible sky's

Laughed as one when tears would disappear into forever oceans of sapphire ink

Leave your windows open you'd say

It only invites adventures

The hardest thing was waking up feeling your side of the bed cold

Knowing the locks had been picked and you spent the night on watch

Smiling I could see your fangs were sharper than the night before

Antonio Montaine - Because we are lucky enough to have sisters

I knew one day your shield would get to heavy
and I knew I couldn't help you carry it

The spells you taught me were old doors too
heavy for me to keep closed

It's better to be alone

The only thing in life I never wanted to share is
burden

It's better to be alone

The only thing in life I never wanted to share is
burden

I never wanted to be alone

Riding on twisted mean iron rails my only
companion memories that haunt like jealous
echo's

Antonio Montaine - Because we are lucky enough to have sisters

That are lost on the breath of impossible night

Let them lie

Let them sing

Those bent burnt spoons polish them until they sparkle like silver oceans

Those wooden benches next to that dirty Yarra we can name them anything we want

And the words you taught me will always be the key to as many adventures as I can imagine

Shua, the poet.
IG - @sutcliffejoshua

Wanted

Shua, the poet. - Wanted

This lonely meadow grows my dissonance.
My search for peace, my lack of change.
While I try to graze, I catch you in hurried glances.
A hunger in your eyes betrays your peace.
I continue to exist in my lonely space but something feels different.
I feel seen.

I am nothing much, just a Deer prancing.
Yet you observe me patiently.
You watch as I move and remark under your breath.
"Such a beautiful creature."
The words may be hollow but to hear them summons tears.
What is beauty to a hunter? Am I ever more than a feast?

Scattered both in mind and soul I summon the energy to run.
I can't allow myself to be starstruck by her grace.
She will make a meal of me. Would I let her?
All my efforts to run are in vain. She has no trouble tracking me.
To be chased has my heart trembling.
Someone who cares where I am.

Shua, the poet. - Wanted

* * * SNAP * ** * *
Steel teeth bite deep into my leg.
She spent time on setting this all up for me.
I saw the trap and didn't hesitate.
Even through this pain her visage flashes through my eyes.
The days of being stalked felt so nice.
As she creeps up to me I hear her whisper
"You won't feel pain for much longer I promise."
It's hard to understand why this makes me feel at ease.
My final moments I have to wonder.
Is my value deemed by what you can take?
Do I love the hunter, or do I just want to be hunted.
And why am I so willing to strip my own flesh to feed others when I am starved?

Thank You

Vibe Union AKA Ry and Myself (Jason) would like to thank all those who have had a hand in shaping Radio Talk into the event it is today,
whether that be previously or currently, the input and effort spent by
everyone will and has always been appreciated.

Radio Bar Fitzroy - @radio_bar - Venue
Pol the Painter - @polthepainter - Illustrator
Porsche Jansuwan @takenbyporsche - Photos
Huich - @huichgoh - Violin
Matt Robb - @mat.robb - Guitar
Jason - @user.name.unknown.jason - Vibe Union/MC
Ry - @rhath_music - Vibe Union/Sound Engineer

We also want to thank all the poets that have contributed to this book: (In order of appearance)

Jason Voss
Izzy (Last Name Redacted)
K.S.K
Vita Mia
Shyaire Ganglani
Mrsk
Jemmi Ongom
Millaa Mercer
Gavi
KrakKen
Xlvi Joon
Kairi Kerr
Hayley
Chris Jayawardena
Lane Milburn
Farhana Muna
Amber Lette
Yaru
M.M. Salavatian
Girl with the Rose Tattoo
Rhath
Antonio Montaine
Shua, the poet.

www.ingramcontent.com/pod-product-compliance
Lightning Source LLC
Chambersburg PA
CBHW062051290426
44109CB00027B/2793